OCCUPIED CITY

Paul van Ostaijen

OCCUPIED CITY

Original Lettering & Illustrations
Oscar Jespers

Translation
David Colmer

Design adaptation
Katy Mawhood

Smoke Stack Books

Smokestack Books
1 Lake Terrace, Grewelthorpe, Ripon HG4 3BU
e-mail: info@smokestack-books.co.uk
www.smokestack-books.co.uk

ISBN 9780992958183

Smokestack Books is represented by Inpress Ltd

Flemish Literature Fund

Smokestack Books gratefully acknowledges the support of the Flemish Literature Fund.

Contributors

David Colmer has translated more than fifty books from Dutch into English, including work by Gerbrand Bakker, Cees Nooteboom and Hugo Claus. He has won several major translation prizes and been shortlisted for several more, including the Popescu Prize and the PEN Award for Poetry in Translation.

Katy Mawhood works as the Fonts Specialist at Oxford University Press. She graduated with distinction from MA Typeface Design, where she developed a keen interest in global writing systems. In her spare time, she freelances as an independent typographer for several publishers.

Grote Zirkus van de H. Geest

heden avond optreden van

Godsdienst & Vorst & Staat!

of het wereldberoemde **TRIO**

luimige **Knock-abouts!!!**

Sukses! Sukses! Lachsukses!!

Dus het wachtwoord voor Oud & JonG!!
is: OPGEPAST. Allen op post in
de Zirkus van de h. Geest!! Allo allo!!
OPtreden van het wereldberoemd TRiO Godsdienst Vorst Staat!

Introduction

Considered one of the most important twentieth-century Flemish poets, Paul van Ostaijen was born in Antwerp in 1896 as the seventh and last child of a Dutch father and a mother from Belgian Limburg. Precocious in both literature and politics, he was expelled from one secondary school and attended two others before starting work as a clerk at the town hall of Antwerp in 1914. His father had sold his successful plumbing business and moved the family to Hove, a rural village just outside of Antwerp, in the previous year and it was from here that Van Ostaijen witnessed the start of the German siege of Antwerp in September, 1914 – including the fire that razed the church of St. Martin in nearby Duffel and the retreat of a long column of Red Cross vehicles, events described in *Occupied City*. Like most other civilians, the Van Ostaijens joined the exodus of refugees, fleeing first to Antwerp and then further north to the Netherlands where they stayed with an uncle in Steenbergen before returning to occupied Antwerp in late October.

Paul van Ostaijen spent the rest of the war in Antwerp, where he plunged into the city's nightlife and cut an extravagant figure in literary and bohemian circles. With the artists Paul Joostens and Floris and Oscar Jespers, he set up a publishing house, Het Sienjaal, where he published his first collections of poetry, while at the same time continuing to write and agitate for a progressive Flemish nationalism. In January 1918 he was sentenced to three months in prison for demonstrating against the pro-Francophone Cardinal Mercier during a procession in Antwerp, but the appeal process delayed the implementation of this sentence until after the war, by which time Van Ostaijen had already fled to Berlin. He remained there for three years, experiencing the disillusionment of the failed Spartacist uprising, mixing with artists and writers (amongst others, those associated with Bauhaus and *Der Sturm*), and producing works including *Occupied City*, which was published in Antwerp before his return to Belgium in May, 1921.

Van Ostaijen avoided imprisonment as he had been granted an 'administrative amnesty', however, he did have to do his military service, stationed in Krefeld in Germany. From the mid-1920s Van Ostaijen suffered increasingly from tuberculosis, the disease that had already claimed two of his siblings, and died of it in 1928 at the age of thirty-two.

From an early age Van Ostaijen read widely in several languages and the rapid evolution of his work reflects international literary developments as well as his own driving poetic vision. *The Signal* (1918) is an early example of humanitarian Expressionism, while *Occupied City*, written during his Berlin exile, is strongly influenced by Dada and August Stramm's 'concentrated word'. Van Ostaijen acknowledged Apollinaire as a source of inspiration, but not for the typography of *Occupied City*, which is intended as a score and not as an illustration of the content of the text. (Some exceptions, such as in the poem 'Zeppelin', reflect an intervention by the designer, Oscar Jespers, who deviated here and in several other places from Van Ostaijen's original manuscript.) In his later work Van Ostaijen moved his emphasis to simplicity and musicality and strove to produce 'pure poetry', autonomous poems that could exist without reference to either their creator or external reality.

Van Ostaijen's work in general and *Occupied City* in particular have long occupied a central and influential position in modern Dutch and Flemish literature, but the language barrier prevented the work from becoming widely known outside of Belgium and the Netherlands. Late translations of *Occupied City* into German (1991) and French (1993) expanded the audience for this key text, and now, a hundred years on from the events it describes, it is a privilege to be able to provide the same service for English speakers. The poet and translator Donald Gardner put it best when he described translating Van Ostaijen as being like 'finding a missing piece of the jigsaw of modernity. It explains modernity and is explained by it.'

David Colmer
Amsterdam 2016

A note on the translation

As a poetic account of Antwerp during World War I, *Occupied City* is as multilingual as the city itself. The original book includes Dutch, in its Flemish variant the language of both the poet and the populace; French, at the time Belgium's administrative language and the language of the bourgeoisie; German, the language of the occupiers; Latin, the language of the Catholic Church; and English, a presence in this cosmopolitan city even then.

Trying to deal with all these languages while making the book accessible to English readers was one of many translation problems. Van Ostaijen quotes songs and advertisements, references films and books, and gives snippets of dialogue in the original languages. In general I have tried to follow him here. Lines of German dialogue represent the occupier, but the significance of the French dialogue is more complicated. Van Ostaijen might be showing the bourgeois background of whoever is speaking, or perhaps satirising Belgian royalism and patriotism. Even when not quoting someone else, he can slip into French now and then, understandable for someone living in a bilingual society, but this can be difficult to follow for an English-speaking reader and these passages I have tended to translate into English.

I have retained Dutch where the poet is quoting from a song or giving the name of a Belgian or Dutch street, ship, book or film.

Now, almost a hundred years after the book was written, it is not always easy to catch the references and I am indebted to the many scholars who have studied Van Ostaijen's work. The books of Robert Snoeck, Jef Bogman and Gerrit Borgers in particular were invaluable. For the identification of typos in the original, I used the errata published as a separate sheet with the first edition and also the comparison of manuscript and book published as an appendix to the *Collected Poems* (1996).

The typography of the book presented a special challenge and it was not always possible to find an English wording that allowed a direct correspondence between the original and the translation. Similarly, some of the changes in English seemed to call for the introduction of new typographical features. Adaptation was required and I did this in collaboration with the designer Katy Mawhood, whose patience, creativity and professionalism were exemplary.

Finally I would like to thank my fellow translators Kiki Coumans and Michele Hutchison for their help with the French, and David McKay for reading the draft translation, saving me from several blunders and providing many invaluable suggestions.

David Colmer
Amsterdam 2016

OCCUPIED CITY

DEDICATION

To Mr Soandso

Much shall be forgiven you
for
you've seen a lot of movies

we know them inside
out
FanTOMas Ligomar with a big L too long

THE IRON PRISON

macaroni films { counts
princesses
apaches }
and

the marvellous Chéri BiBi

f a t a *l i* t a s

« Dieppe o mon pays natal je t'ai quitté en forçat; vicomte je te revois »
or
« je croyais m'être mis dans la peau d'un honnête homme; ME voilà dans celle d'un assassin. »

God the Father presents the final act

director archangel Michael
planes blockade submarines strange races
the beginning of the end
the breast has been drained
the child throws away the bottle
nursemaids – cry

The Last of the MoHicans

is the most appropriate novel
all tried and tested
we have come to the end of all isms schisms
all cathedrals
all prophets
all pulpits
struck dumb
with the only positive
being done with it every man jack
jack joe john

N ihil in every direction
ihil in every family
ihil in every language and
every dialect
NIHIL in every symbol

rotating
nihil

n i h i l in saltire

N I H I L in crux suastika

Nihil in vagina

Zut building cathedrals and shelling them

blaming others

naturally

citron nature

others make babies
vows of chastity are cheap

buggered and
blasted if we'll give
bishops generals statisticians the satisfaction
of counting children
Deo Gratias

amen

and children born by misfortune or chance can only be taught
self defence

rotating *nihil*

square nihil

triangular **n i h i l**

pyramidal NIHIL

your moral the one plausible thing for us

to do

trains tapping out the tired

rhythm

of

weary

people.

Positive is convincing oneself
of emptiness
of mud and clay
of ruination
the realisation of complete emptiness

echoing

idealistic slogans

emptiness lungs hollow body lying
hollow lungs echoing aimlessly inside
let the ministers priests generals make babies
turn around turn around turn around again
rotating earth reversed

a A A

omega

◊ ◊

Rimmel's New Cosmetique

For fixing the Hair Whiskers or Mustachios
and giving them a beautiful gloss & natural black
or brown colour.

E Rimmel, Parfumer 79 Strand; Bld. des Capucines, Paris

◊ ◊

Du rouge pour les lèvres

D
O
R
I
N

if the pageant rolls out again
the pageant again
the Ommegang
omega
omicron
Alpha (the letter not the margarine) beta zeta eta theta

t ê t e

à

cou
per

I want to be the director
Bayard Giant Giantess scrapped
only our
heroic ideals
burlesque costumes

{ honesty in top hat and dress coat
religion tiara cardinal red
metaphysics with little angel's wings

and

PINNACLE

O Susanna waaas ist das **LE** –

ils en ont tant goûté
qu'ils en ont dégueulé

We have known all songs 3 Walzertraum evolution
in three languages

from Lustige Witwe to Czardasfürstin
strike out all syrupy operettas
sentimental ersatz songs

Tango RRRouge

Dans mon pays English tune French lyrics

quand je suis gri-
se

rue de la Glaciè___________re

ICH TANZ
so
gern TANGO O BUENOS AIRES

Sous le ciel de l'Argentine
leaving only counterpoint to JAZZ BAND
6 in the morning grey street
FRERE JACQUES
FRERE JACQUES
frère Jacques
lève-toi
tines
sonne les ma
les matines
sonne
everything is empty
frère Jacques
the last Pernod
Picon

hollow sea wreck
never mind
stinking bus down worn-out street
lazy trains through stinking country
mountains sea valley   valley sea mountains
sea   sea   sea
wreck

lazy trains

sozzled

rigolo gigolo zigoto
si tu veux faire une petite ballade
you've balladeered your way through Europe
your expectations die
Utah Indians Aztecs

PLACE BLANCHE

and not the least of your achievements
inventor of a map

EUROPE   according to   EROTIC BEDDINGS
we have known Europe for so long so long
drawn-out stretching flat and upwards
geologically
river basins
politically
religiously
commercially
and taking all of that and all of that
                    into consideration
this   EROTIC MAP   is a necessity
soon Privatdozenten
will lecture university classes
on this innovation in the service of mankind
on Corfu the women are so

legs thighs breasts Berlin **Germany** BRUSSELS Amsterdam
Bucharest London Paris hair perfume fleurs Houbigant Longchamp
Maisons-Laffitte joe jack john joker gigolo rubsters **ehrliche Frau**

and for five minutes you have seen
the necropolis
of the Acropolis

more than enough

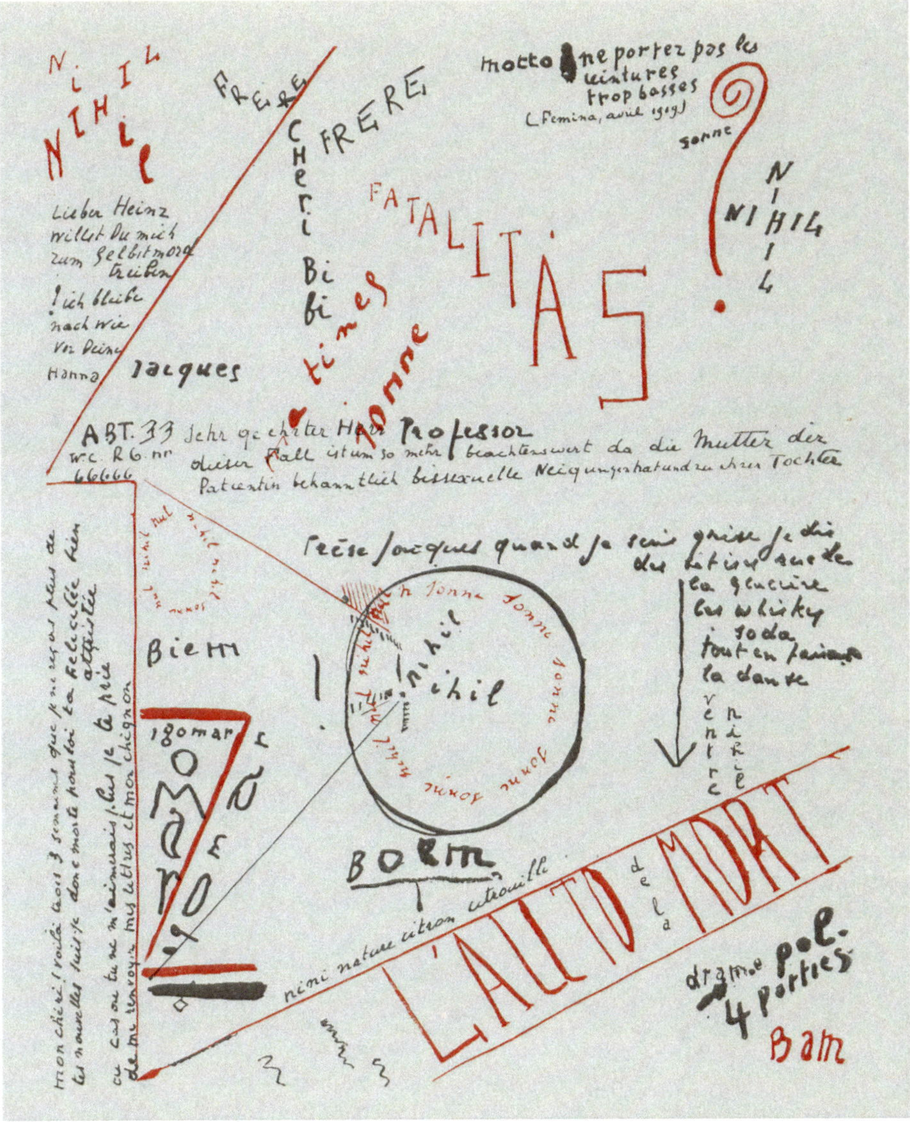

NIHIL
FRERE
CHERI
FRERE
motto ne porter pas les ceintures trop basses
(Femina, avril 1919)
sonne
NIHIL
Lieber Heinz willst Du mich zum Selbstmord treiben
! ich bleibe nach wie vor Deine
Hanna
Jacques
FATALITAS
Bi bi
times
sonne
ABT. 33 W.C. R6. nr 66.666
Sehr geehrter Herr Professor
dieser Fall ist um so mehr beachtenswert da die Mutter der Patientin bekanntlich bisexuelle Neigungen hat und zu ihrer Tochter
Biem
nihil
sonne sonne sonne sonne
Bom
nini nature citron citrouille
dramme pol. 4 parties
Bam
L'ALTO de la MORT
ventre

Should they have fallen all cathedrals
cannibals
Hannibals generals
ideals
colonels
brothels
perhaps
there will be room
for a beauty that speaks for itself
undefiled
unknown

if **It** is not destroyed
once and forever
standing pure

cleansing earth
vermin weeds

perhaps one day we will say j'ai soupé
d'en avoir soupé

Nihil
these ordinary words
return to the essence

prison letters
ordinary word-wounds
a human's simple stuttering for love

and all this grey cell
not the whole miserable life
of mournful people longing thistles

and are these cross-drawn countries
not one great Christ
full of hollow wounds

and this hollow echoing sense of
despondency
not like Good Friday once

7-10 Aug. 1920

THREATENED CITY

Visé march Liège mortars
march mortars
Puppchen Du bist mein Augenstern
Puppchen mein liebes Puppchen **Heil Dir im Siegerkranz**
March-past through Brussels all day and all night

A r m e e v o n K l u c k
Jef Jef Jef 'ne Zeppelin
kruipt al gauw de kelder in

eins zwei eins zwei eins zwei eins zwei
Prussian Prussian
march mortars

We're standing my brother les hommes au balcon

the flickering hoRIzon
the distant tower and blazing FIRe
the spaSMs of the tramPLed army
the *Masochistic march*

the d e b a c l e

the dust of summer

the sludge of autumn

country road 200 Red Cross vehicles
night spl it by 200 cars
200 **S**irens_______!
a thousand bURSts of shrapnel
around the blazing tower
going up in Flame
and the refugees the endless fleeing throng
and the cattle find it damned unpleasant
and the lice hitching a ride
and all of that and all of that
till morning **came**
Puppchen Du bist mein Augenstern

The pa**C**ing **C**ity
the forts will hold they'll fall they'll hold they'll fall
the pa**C**ing fearful **C**ity

growing desire

the camp followers withdraw to the fortified city

All the whores of the whole country
and they do well it does the trick
along the boulevards
the bright boulevards the teeming boulevards
in the evening **PRUSSIAN BLUE** *light* from *white* fox
big shots in red fox
fear and desire

what will

tomorrow bring

the paperboys forts will hold

The gravely threatened city we will defend to the bitter end
lies trembling pale-bodied
an ASHEN POOL in the evening PRUSSIAN BLUE and the *danger*
stops time stops pan ting time stops space

still

until

it goes

bang

bang bang crump crackle crumping crackle crash
air displacement in **Zut** major
and counterpoint people
Their displacement in Zut minor
bombs bang
and the crump thumps into a house (record express delivery)

house in flames
flickering flames in front of moon
moon in Flames

flame

moon

FLAMES

The ciTy STands STill
as if the city's strings have been cut

and all the dancers staggered in their mad circle

are we or are we performing a macabre play
for the salon-goers of the 18th
only the SHELLS are positive
city theatre harlequins

Halley's comet
besieged city
hurry up gentlemen 15 minutes left
just enough
cash
the generals pimps patriots the demimonde
the goose flesh of the demimonde that's no advertisement
that's not satin not silk not moire
that's goose flesh
shells falling despite your cash charity

SHELLS
            falling
                        falling
                                    falling
                                                drip

cannon coitus

ça và ça viens ça viens *ça va*
a brothel flees to the cellar
bouncing breasts football bellies
tulle gold silver voile Mimi Manon sequins and teeth
the madam up to the nines
no time to change
the shell falls
                    without
                              un client mesdames voyons

in the cellar flesh quivers by the kilo
quivering breasts quaking bellies shuddering thighs
paint streams on greased mugs full of fear
and the grotesque oriental splendour
tulle   sequins
scientific progress
teeth chattering   gold and lead this time
Gaby - Recamier   no dough to flee
suit way out of style streetwalking impossible
Ah c'est la merde merde pour les Boches merde pour tout le monde
lanky Irène is especially cold silver snakeskin mesh

and

watch out for rats

brothel Screams! girls huddle together
next door an abandoned piano

oh oh si vous voulez l'amour *profitez des beaux jours*

c'est le **MOMENT** qui

NOW racing cars - fleeing - flight
growing through the
piercing C
bolts I
glowing T
Y

wrecks cars riPping dark swathes of night
wrecked writhing

irregular TWITCHING **crushed people**
caked soldiers **cursed beasts**

cursed

crushed

caked

masochistic march

steps drinking the street

thirst-burning steps drinking dryness

treading tramping treading tramping

CORPSE rUMbling rusty cannon

MACA**BR**e RiBs

DANCE iron

RATtling ribs claTTERring COBBLED ROADS

dropping

and

marauders break into houses lighter than shells

philanthropy

rescuing heirlooms

Rattling   crawling   fleeing
crushed army
streams of cars   yelling   yellow   light

a bus slashing past   **OLD TOM GIN**   straitened street
transport   trucks   trailers
machine guns   cannon
Bones   **B**reaking   *R*attling   *R*ibs

fleeing   ling
cr   awl

!

Screaming staff car   sirens scream light
stripe in
treacle
night

r_i_n_g

corpses strewn around the city

LE

ARMS   **gs**   waving arms

trea   ding   le   GS   not   making   progress

have they forgotten something at the line of defence
not the king the first soldier in the first trench
still there
or his steel helmet
Good Lord maybe they forgot the king
or his steel helmet
and tomorrow he's being snapped with his steel helmet
for new stamps
seasick prime minister

Grey

greying grey day
growing grey exodus
Goodbye threatened city
refuge north
annual fair
carousel
people and things
pram
hatbox
lamp chimney
the same things for hours
has God forsaken this nation

the whores forget to solicit

they only flee
as if one can't do both flee and solicit
but
the chairman of the ESTAMINET UNION saves the day
his top hat
and his tricolour neckerchief
EENDRACHT MAAKT MACHT
DIEU PROTÈGE LES ESTAMINETS
silver letters
the crowd is a sight

Valse len te

you can use their heads as stepping stones
couldn't that have stayed symbolic
treading
kilometre counting
kilogram
kilolitre (seldom used)
kilowatt
kilokwatt
kilokwatta

PRIDE OF THE NETHERLANDS

Kwatta = de Ruijter + 2 Tromp + 2 de Wit
stolen from me

B. S. A.

Birmingham Small Arms

3 fusils
a beauty the family's pride and joy
Always pram hatbox lamp chimney babe in arms

the most beautiful fair **EX**
OD
US

Always people
a peculiar puppet show put on by God the Father
or Siderius (for astrologists)

Fleeing tykes
fleeing people
Fleeing army
the 3 ages flee

Canaan
in
re
verse

defeated army

victorious army

around the city people everywhere
empty city
long roads of people
tell me the songs and I will tell you
whether
you are leaving the city or won

march mortars
Puppchen mein liebes Puppchen
Privatdozenten missing-link faces
provincial outpouring - Pomeranian oafs
Oberleutnant zum Befehl
Puppchen
immer Puppchen
eins zwei eins zwei eins zwei eins zwei

DREI

what who Donnerwetter who
had the gall to
eins zwei eins zwei eins zwei
KAISER (not the motorcycle racer)
G o t t m i t u n s

Gott
mit
uns

PARIS is on the other side of the river
Kultur Tradition du Volnay 69
es lebe der Kaiser
der jute jott

crushed

march

!SIEG!

E
X
O
D
U
S

The CRUMP over the CITY

always elegant
Mr Crump Esq.
very fast car
greeting everyone
alighting calmly
at his hotel

Marching foreign soldiers
occupied country occupied city aerial view

KODAK

Teeming
spreading like an oil slick
starting small
developing in geometric progression
first town
2 4 16
all towns
all villages
all hamlets
all farms

repulsive poles

fleeing and taking
the city still there
untouched island
in the slick
but
on maps and over town halls everywhere foreign flags

are flying

If a country pours all of its legs
if a country pours all of its arms
all of its arsenals
all of its copper iron tin
all of its uniform buttons
all it can find
if a country pours
spewing everything
spewing over
over-straining
Seizing with
over-open-strained arms
Crack of officers' whips
splash
splat
splashing
Dance through the land of Howitzers
Dance of the crumps
shrapnel minuet
machine-gun heart attack
Austrian 32
Imperial 42
racing straight at the goal
across the country

overwhelming
aRsenals RaTTling across the country

Oh!

a candle snaps
falls over
has fallen

city

now
the slick is
everywhere

soldiers walking
soldiers striding
soldiers singing
drumrolls

VICTORY
foreign victory
fallen city
soldiers walking flowery rifles
soldiers striding flowery rifles
soldiers singing victory
through the empty
city

sieg

all the soldiers
all the mutilated
all the dead
field hospital
fluttering flags
conquering flags
flags conquering the city
flags taking buildings
flags taking the TOWER
foreign army Growing in empty city
drumming marching military backs left-right left-right
entering the city
silent
the foreign army fills streets
foreign flags
foreign voices
foreign [3]
across the country
across the city
forms
signs

Garnisonverwaltung

FELDLAZARETT

3 ETAPP. KOMM.

Off. Kas. 4 Reg. Bielef.

Off. messe

❦❦❦❦❦❦❦❦❦
SOLDATENHEIM
❦❦❦❦❦❦❦❦❦

conquering houses city country
smashed anthill
people flee
into backrooms
blind blinds

BEKANNTMACHUNG

All citizens are required to

Der Platzkommandant

the foreign words d a *on the*
n
c e noticeboards

The Occupation

be
gins

Abandoned Forts

Abandoned forts
and
rancid grass
under constant rustling rain

TRAPPED by the sky
stinking puddle decomposing **shako**
CORPSE sprawled in maggots crawling
with maggots
falling
corpse
mute Scream of shako raining
s k y
filthy bubbles oozing from oilskin
trampled barbed wire

|c u t s|
|hands|

and bleeds gushes filth with filthy rain
mute stumps abandoned abatis
thousand **1,000** **1,000**
dizzy
shuddering cellar skeletons cold earth
blasted brewery one wall standing

BESTE   EXTRA   DOBBELE

snapped signpost

reddish-brown Instructions

about what

about what   the rain

unending

filth gushes

Rusting   ironware

steel helmet   chopped   o f f   head

broken wheel

HEIGHT shriek GUN BARREL   halting

4th DIV. ARM.

rust urine pus filthy caked muck

lying   f a l l e n

fort

abandoned

giant helmet redoubt dome

rain

space

rain

space

dejection

Lonely City

WHO-WHO

shrieking lunatic

wind

only

still

street

city

Night

it is the rain falling in fine drops
it is the rain

it is
the
rain

HOLLE HAVEN

Hollow Harbour

Hollow harbour
hollow swelling waves
always   the same time
slapping   trestles   dyke
empty water playing
                    and
into the distance
hollow   harbour   hollow   markets

Shuddering skeleton rattling trestles
Hooves clacking
Just one – only – echoing
        That
        Aimless falling
cell walls sky
always the steps of just one person
                    just one wagon

If only the walls moved red-hot story by **Poe**

Abandoned dolmen
stuffed mammoth
sudden wilderness
suddenly

Pompeii Herculaneum
missing only all-too-modern means of transport to get around

in the Museum of Arts and Crafts
Kunsten en Ambachten
hollow harbour found in the year O. L. J. C. 1914
ANNO MCMXIV
simulating operations with several wax dummies
the docker the tally clerk the dock constable
blue coat with silver trim
WAXWORKS window number
and improved version of the galley slaves of Cayenne
annual fair younger years fascinated by galley slaves Nos. 3 and 7
and by the Garde - Chiourme
hollow harbour entirely relocated as an attraction for the forthcoming

!WORLD EXPOSITION! in MILWAuKeE

(They'll have to ban the Hun)

YOU no longer have the lyrical dynamism of tentacular memory
Those born in a port want to die there and nowhere else
so it's said
(the painter Dupuys left Paris longing for le HÂVRE)
Carcasses   Caulking   Hammering the delicately arched
hull elegant bow
much flatter than half an orange
the   hoL   Low   sound
but
captured in the Loud vibrations around
thousandfold e__________cho / under   metallic   dome
lesson in French diction

leurs
lourds marteaux
tombent en cadence domptent les métaux
(for the occasion that is very good)

Caulking carcasses
hammering
metallic dome
inverted cauldron
clear clatter of scattered skittles
transatlantic hull harbour-half
balance opposite side : the Rest
brown sloBBy hoBByhorse lost house crooked wheels port train

A
P
L
A
N
D

sails front and wings
Floris Jespers saw this transatlantic
harbour half sharply
but the brown slobby hobbyhorse
is the perfect colouristic
to transition
the caulking-tar pigment
and the whole olfactory mal
a gam

river freshness tar caulking
and the caustic
hides bales wool

(hou s es falling FARWEST stands cowboy trick photo)

oil Oil-Nuts cocoNuts lubricating Oil
our { national / colonial } product
flotte petit drapeau
Ivory Ivory Market
and all things reminiscent of
sudden little clouds
guano

CapetowN CongO CairO PATAGONIA

the big signs
the English words and English accent of the harbour patois

D I S P A C H E

NORDDEUTSCHERLLOYD

LORELEY

ZUM HALBEN KILO

Tabakos
Themistokles
Chyriadis

NORDISK
FLACKE

Steels &
Iron

Shelter 68 Uruguay
hangar
shed
Kattendijk Z W
petrol tank 7

R. S. L. **Rio Janeiro** LIEBIG Uruguay

LAPLAND Tinto Great EAstern R

First class with all the modern comforts

ANTWERP- HARWICH-
Liverpool-
NEW YORK

MUSIC
DANCING
GIRLS

SHIPPING MASTER

good-bye
whole
casks of freedom

Floris Jespers has captured this
giving it an equivalent on canvas
that evokes the sensation of smelling
caulking tar to bales of hides
earthy colours that cut through all senses

With the harbour whole I saw cobbles moving in all directions
leaping
to the beat of the harbour's heart

grey strip
magic wand
only the husk of all that left
completely   H ollow   H arbour
from the busy shipping before
upturned basin

all fULLness fALLs

idLe aLLeys aLong the harbour

empty
raTTling sign *The City of New York*
gone
BLACK JACK
still lifes of broken signs

Zum HALB MAXI oncert *estam* ELEY Shippi

KI café c M ng

LO
master *inet*

electric piano erotic whinnying

ban
a don
ed

PA
spirits
LE ALE

idle alleys lining h o l l o w
h a r b o u r

Transatlantic surrogate lighter
C. R. B.
abandoned steamer hulk

G N E I S E N
A U

Es ist verboten zu betreten
die Hafenkommandantur
KARTHAGO

yet
Bull and it's my father and I'm going
Mississippi River

and
BLACK WHITE
WHISKY

Museum fortress city centre
these antiquities
harbour Carthage folklore

OLD CURIOSITY SHOP

Corner boats
splash of water
and rolling
Elvire
Anna
Marguerite
Dynamo
Mobile
Ma Poupoule
Corner boats small rigging
seen from close-by and compressed
river and boats asymmetric relationship
Paul Joostens painted the boats and the flatness of their hulls
small crowded corner of hollow harbour
thinking at once harbour
painting
harbour pure forms

Suddenly halted iron construction
no-longer-clanging
loud howls of idle cranes and / silent
b u r i e d c i t y

stammering lone li ness prayer
pointless tall skeletons
small cruiser on the river rolling pompously
stupid thing

broken carcass
port whores staring hopelessly
Feldgrau poor substitute for princely sailors
where are the old days
Hopeless cranes
Howling Whinnying
falling barren
Rusty locks screech
wild WHO-WHOing birds of prey
endless distance hoarse cranes
quays
docks
alleys
hull
Piano stops
HalT! „ Hier gehts zum Sammelpunkt der tapferen Feldgrauen „
poor fallen alley
irony
former princess
nordisk city
or at Dutch Kee's
streetwalkers lay soiled flowers by the Christ of the Dyke
Wilderness with withered cranes
C rump city centre moved to
a few boulevard cafés cinemas
H Howling Huddling Hollow Harbour
PALE ALE sleeping
beauty

Brothel

Sprawled worn-out brothels
e m a c i a t e d
YOO-HOO! Steinlen
in a filthy pubic triangle
rain and darkness
and a policeman
occupied-city-brothel-street
dank rotting fruit
reeking
from a greengrocer's
grimy violet

The madam says
je regrette monsieur
à la guerre comme à la guerre
BEFORE ?   – yes before !
              but now
c'est si difficile monsieur
and the gentleman in the top hat says
Vous perdrez votre bonne clientèle

back from { Bapaume
Noyon
the Chemin des Dames

s l i r l n u
o d e s i e p

as if for ration books
(man does not live by bread alone)

! HIER ! schöne *junge* mäd chen

Eh là-bas Väterchen
par ici →

The policeman maintains order
no pushing
Who is at the end here

from 4

to

4

ZEPPELIN

Newspapers

ZEPPELIN
LONDON

good bye Piccadilly
SQUARE
farewell Leicester

BEATA INSULA

Empty Cinema

sentiment and film
empty cinema
the Lonely Bench
the Diabolical Woman
the Poor Girl from Belleville

Nod ding

pianist plunking away
plunking through to the end

z______________________**A**

to a gallop
some warmed-up
beans
warmed-up beans
warmed-up beans
beans
beans

Nomenclature of Deserted Things

deserted EXISTENCE
deserted city
deserted square
deserted cinema
                                        cinema cracked coffee cup
hollow harbour
hollow people
weary people
tired people
tired trains
                                        jolting jarring standstill sown in landscape
deserted buffet
deserted bar
deserted barman
deserted barmaid
UPRIGHT PUPPETS
                                        dejection deserted   **BAR**
feeble morning
tired noon
faint evening
naked night
houred rosary   trolley
                                        broken   tram   s   topped
                                                                  silent

feeble church
faint candles
dozing choir
swaying people
swaying prayer

hollow and deserted
faint and feeble
dozing swaying
shuffling soldiers
foreign street

tired weary p e o p l e
1,000 fronts too many

City Still Life

Last vignette on a catchpenny paper
e.g. all vignettes light
red pink yellow royal blue
the last vignette a heavy lump of black
or darkness

iridescent green showing fast fall into dirty oxide green
last vignette stiffening motionless
the text below relates deserted castle wicked fairy success
the whole story
and all the happy colours above
damsels pages orange and penny-chocolate pink
are dragged
Destroyed
weight of the dark corner lower right
Child unmans me fear and horror of the dark squ
are
that whole catchpenny print
lying

deserted
there city city
deserted

Outlandish houses in occupied city
deserted city of a thousand and one nights
deep violet night all houses
oriental style

or are they giant cakes Youth
at the caliph parties of my
representing the newly conquered city
two tall cakes and the street is the table
the guests have disappeared
and now this mute cake-table stands in the night

A bove the table hangs an arc lamp

and now these cakes backlit

a flat set piece

(the evil spirit catchpenny print did not forget this last lamp
DELIBERATE: desolation needs this misplaced lighting)

O n e S t ep
fugit irrepara bile
is the forgotten eunuch at this Caliph feast

Above in the VIolet sky

dark violET

phosphoresces

YEllow

HAnD

fiVe very clear

5 FIngers

Dead Sunday

Sunday
r
o
s
a
r
i
e
s
the minutes it cannot fill unfillable

the **TRAM still** stopped hollow
Sunday
empty space

people stand alone
lost dr
opped
rosary beads
the tram detonates the everyday
consecrated Sunday tolling
mothballs and bourgeois women

the sharp
edge of
a dull
Sunday

no **D**estination

only

tightRope walKers

the **D**ull **D**ance of the trams on

m__y____h_i_g_h________________w__ire___________nerves

stretched-out nerves

dance to the music

of dry drear y

r

o

s

a

r

y

b

e

a d s

minutes

Sous les Ponts de Paris

A cry goes up from all the places
they have put You on display   Your pain

They have hung You up on the corner of every block
to catch pennies in an offertory box

Still with the people You commune
they plunge their arms into your wounds

We put our hands in Your warm wounds We are deaf
and blind in faithlessness

Your Corpse has been defiled by popes and priests
Your wounds have taught our hands belief

They have raised up churches like mighty halls
Silver and gold drip from the walls

Our faith is so small and so weak
like the flame that dances at your feet

You are displayed on every corner HARLEQUIN
with your beaten attitude and Your suffering

Among us again in all Your statues You are one
with the occupied city Your weeping wears away the stone

Under your statue I know the water from the downpipe
wears away the stone but that too is Your sorrow

You are reincarnate among us
tormented Harlequin Your Mother a sob-wracked sloven

We cannot see God but as a Harlequin
our times are so full of pain and suffering

2

Your final incarnation is for the rabble alone
I saw You deserting from the front

They did not gather up the weapons You cast aside
Holy Deserter, those relics were not convenient

In such times all churches should display
Your deserter's guise and the weapons You threw away

I saw You staggering from town to occupied town
weak worn-out nerve-wracked and beaten down

In my occupied city I have seen You often
when You walked into the dance hall the music stopped

its slow waltz the rhythm of Your face was SO
much stronger in its sorrow than a broken cello

and the gigolos and bar girls danced their slow light WALTZ
to the sorrowful rhythm of Your FACE

I saw You standing in a stinking alley
a Landsturm man to keep you company

You moved amongst the press-ganged unemployed
long trains to Germany full of ragged men and half-grown boys

You kept watch on top of the dyke
with cold streetwalkers through the rainy night

Now You are worn-down and exhausted
stuffed full of sorrow once more

Rain drips from Your filthy sopping beards of hemp

over   the   city

Dripping down with the rain on the city's filth
Your halting rhythm

CITY OF GRIEF

AERIAL ATTACKS

Civilian sirens must be

notified

1
2 { darkness everywhere
3

Light in the room tints flickering violet to Black
on linen and paper
cafés =
unmoving armoured cars
light artillery
all windows see street through coloured glass
windows like German professors
blue-black sinking of extinguished things

Filling

deeper **DARK**ness **d**im **d**ismal street

Falling

dismal
i s
darkness
Prussian blue
eddying
black

the tram slides movement that

is

d
e
a
d

mask

Oh

mask
to
wards
me

!

together
with

I
AM
THE
STREET

street
Scream } ME
tram

noiseless

scream falls

Spectral **S**treet
reflecting
me myself

if I were
Scared

Fear

would not be

Dark Driving Deeper into Darkness
blinDfolDed tram Driving

white gloves

S c reaming

alone
in the
street

mist

streetlamps creating velvet surround

dancing corona

darkness surrounds

light

trams creating their darkness around them

darkness sliding along with light

less noise

senses simultaneous

the ear hears – the noiselessness –

the eye Sees

noiselessness light moving through mist

velvet

st_rai_ned n_er_ves
mist breaking
over them
creak of trolleys
muffled crackling

light opals
press **Lead** oN treaD
pearls beaTing
the streeT

muffled echoes in mist
velvet carriage **R A G**

R A G T I M E

around the corner

down the street

the doorman

warm light
smell of guitars
sound of whisky and
wilted rose

your flower Musette

if it's miserable outside

it's lovely near you

because

Jaarsma

warms well

Banal dance

Life screams
life seizes

and life
falls
CracK
crazed draping one-step

DANCE of desire

M agic chain things outside
we walk and want to run
and vice versa

and life
falls
al ways

Nonstop dancehall
standing and not knowing
lights dimmed
we stand there amazed

AH! YOO-HOO!

and DANCE
life
falls

Wanting crazed draping
lungs let us down
hair turns grey mid-dance
still standing among young girls
dancing on over our
FALL

Knowing nothing of reality
dreaming through streets standing
and our dreamt nights are clear
full of festivity
a little semblance a little being
bare trees
or violins or banjos

CONSUMED IN AN unKNOWN GLOW

BANJO

B
A
BANJO
J
O

says CRACK

and the

doctor heart attACK

House City Me.

(Mother few words
circling brother's absence)
My brother comes
at night
S sits down with us
says nothing
so often silence

house

or I lie exhausted
in her words

rolling ships and safe **haven**

L E T T E R .

all the doors slam
a procession enters the house
racing upstairs
Letter into the room

He is **everywhere now**

flesh and blood
HIS hand holding *letter*
the whole house a beating pulse LETTER

house sleeps again
day night
house sleeps
and
no Orange
breaks Violet
shadows falling in the house

Not dusting blinds
bro K en - hearted - H ouse street shadowing
broken - hearted - street city

counting count time time in this breathless

this pacing empty room
Oh this pacing of
Breath-empty Oh this not feeling
Pacing RUIN house
street
city

Good News

Good news from the front
immediately received W T by
the Ladies of Christian Charity (motto mine is mine)
a whole battalion of Feldgrauen
the King alone in the trench
Does he flee ? a king does not flee (very true)
Samson he takes the jawbone of an ass
Smites ½ battalion
the other 50 % turns tail
He then cleanses the jawbone of Boche blood
it was a battalion from SAXE-COBURG-GOTHA

In the adjoining trench stands the Crown Prince
also alone
a smaller group of enemies approaches
and is crushed too to a lesser degree (proportion)
Respectful all the same
the Boches withdrew
Why ?
They were Bavarians Es lebe Wittelsbach
Eisner!

The Charlatan up on his Stand
delivers patter to the Land.

Great Circus of the Holy Ghost

performing this evening

Religion &
Sovereign & State!

the world-famous TRIO

of jolly **Knockabouts!!!**

Success! Success! Comic success!!

The watchword for Young & Old!!

IS: **ATTENTION. Everyone at their post in the Circus of the Holy Ghost!! Allo âllo!!**

PERformance by the renowned **TRIO!** Religion Sovereign State!

The Inward Circles

Music Hall

1

THEN

inside the circle of her despondency
the city began to
live

Music Hall full
of
vague
desire
in its electric frugality
people in suspense
before the banal wonder

Music Hall a balloon
a
b
o
u
t

t
o

burst

Step inside Drama in full swing
orchestra **Luigini ballet égyptien**
(music that is always a half beat too late
it *follows* the dance)

Luigini drama in full battle
filmgoer pay attention to the music and
you know what the film is up to

learn the dictionary of film music

no magic
you don't need to watch the film
music tells exactly

The sickly youth in spring
loveache dept.
= { Pourquoi me REVEILLER
Oh Oh Oh souffle du
Oh printemps **AN**

fatal love = Ridi Pagliaccio

true love, self-sacrifice
1 rich + 1 poor
{ = mais
le plus joli rêve

quiet wistfulness = German music

LA TRAVIATA = mounting { fire or ardour

the great GIUSEPPE VERDI

HISTORICAL FILM = { Jerusalem
the march of the Huguenots
L'Africaine

TRIUMPH = { ce matin
oric
hist
j'ai vu dans le lointain

JOCKEY's triumphal procession
or = { A I D A march
blazing passion in march tempo

development of the conflict drama tragedy expression direction { **SAMSON**

and

DELILAH

orchestral triumph is

blazing { fire passion love ardour

UNTIL

standing

climbing rising bass cello violin the conductor is UP on his chair

and

the music______________________________

BOOM

KETTLEDRUM

everything **FLAT**

Oh________________________**O**h

racing again violins cellos basses brass triangle

drums KETTLEDRUMS

racing running racing running racing RUNNING

STOP!

drama in full battle tarts snakes throwing themselves at honourable gentlemen the family falters the factory falters honour falters lies there all ideas go tumbling DOWN

HALT!

3

legs arms move room ruffle

A-C-R-O-B-A-T-S

competition

climbing

cornet

drum

feet

hands

climbing

rings drums rumbling

bars

in the hall

drums rumbling

in the hall

ropes

Acrobats rolling drum

legs

arms

legs

arms

ladders

up and

climbing falling from

drumroll ladders

KETTLEDRUM

et voilà smile

Drum and acrobats One

Drums roll drums rumble

drums thrum

BOM **BAM**

O -

r--a--n--g--e a-c-r-o-b-a-t-s

tee tee hEE

blossoming bloom blown

SPLASH

tarita tarita taritatta

a wave goes through the hall
rolls through the hall
sloshes against the hall walls

growing sloshing **rolling**

rumbling drums ladders space and time

trembling rustling rolling rolling
tensing
clenching
fists and
hands and
hands that SLAP

tensing swelling bottoms swelling bottoms swelling tensing
ROUND

rolls swish rustles rumbles everyone
a-c-r-o-b-a-t-s
DRUM
hands that SLAP

Coffee **C**ups **D**ancing Along With The **C**row**D**

d
an
swir ling ce

l et go

tinkling dome-breaking glasses

stiff standing

5

Iron claw
pressing down
on cinema dome

and the people twist their fists and
tense their shoulders
against
the cinema dome
the Iron Claw

posters
changing to

Menacing Torment

the cops the cops!

come little Jeanne
Coco
hear your heart
your blood
your sinking away

everything around you sinking away
and only
the raging rattling of your flick
your dynamo
your heart

quand je suis grise

the rocking of the barge
that founders
that sinks
that goes down
sunk

THE CLUTCHING HAND

Jeanne
me
the others
ragged
vagabonds

Asta Nielsen

for Paul Joostens

ASTA NIELSEN
ASTA
astra
star
empress Our Lady
Our Lady of Denmark
we carry you under baldachins

broad HOST

You

A
S
T
A

The greatest consolation for weary people
official reports Paris London Berlin Petrograd Rome
day in day out
rosary of reports
litany of dying cigarettes
when darkness emerges from light
and light from darkness
Thunderbolt
Starring ASta NIElsen
Queen of the Stock Exchange lady Eskimono first-class Carmen
DEATH in Seville
I still see the swing of your hips
beautiful with the camera movements
and your mouth
and your teeth biting the limp flower

the drop of your hands
says
so much
and
the way you appear
vous *Voilà!*
ASTA
astra
happy humanity
Felicitée
poupée
ma bien-aimée

You have a way of entering
and gone
zIP!
too fast for the cameraman
and the screen in constant harmony
while *you* are on it
immanent CINEMATIC EQUILIBRIUM

therefore his prayer must be
A S T A
YOU

immaculate cinematic balance

N
I
E
L
S
E
N

pray for us
poor cinema-goers
the purity of limp hands dropping
pray for us weary people
the hearty laughter of a Sébasto whore
pray for us faded loins
smiling into a rainbow aperitif
pray for us men with no refreshment
ASTA more than all the stars together
pray for us who can manage without stars
asta more than the sun
since the invention of electricity
ASTA more than the moon
since loving couples became mere WAXWORKS
asta pray for us
without sun moon or stars
but not without cinema limp hands and aperitifs

C
I
N
E
M
A

asta deliver us from misfortune
Bad luck at the races

asta deliver us from sentimentality

but give us the Objectivity of your poised feet
ASTA deliver us
from gaslights in this age
of electricity

ASTA give us a kind gesture
and
keep acting in CINEMA
keep playing with your feet
but not with Ours

DE vi
ma
PROFundis cla

this is no fantasy
YOU sustain us
more than Schopenhauer Bergson and the Farmer's Union

Asta great passive A s t a
without sentiment
simply
swaying on a donkey's back
l'apéro sur le sébasto
your broad face
your wide mouth

a s t r a

s
e
n
s
a

F
I
L
M

w
i
t
h

A
S

burst cherry of objective sensuality
bloody wound across your face
because you are very well made-up
black eyes

nothing suits you so well as black eyes
white fox as vulgar as it gets
black-and-white robe retroussée
CONTRASTS

AStA you
living image of struggle we
will he get up
will he be lost
two boxers fighting in each of us
the boxer for **A**
the **Z** boxer
and in the end the winner by mighty knockout is
always **Z** the end the debacle

Z

Asta we box for you
blood dripping from our faces
this sacrifice is not enough
drink
our
blood
apéro
sur
le
sébasto

A

You are a good woman
with cheap tickets
you are everyone given individual imagination
that's what I call   the progress   of science
the multiplication of woman
PAUL JOOSTENS
You and me coffee and cigarettes
and still able to afford
the sidereal oscillation of Asta's legs
rigolo
apéro
sébasto
ASTA can do it all

Look
hola
night
blue
there she is it's ASTA our ASTA ASTRA our asta astra astra nielsen
wallet lifter
elle s'approche sans méfiance
et tout à coup elle s'élance
slightly different
more imagination

queen of the stock exchange with
sudden weakness for artiste
she becomes Spanish
such an enormous harem in this one ASTA
don't you agree Paul J ?
I do Paul van O
she is so much so infinitely much
the many in one
the one in many
she is the gnostic par excellence

she is

ASTA

astra

Voilà!

hip
tip
top

And so we sit sight sated
washed
by the waves of your divine acting
while the war news rolls over us
Berlin Paris London Petrograd

h
i
p

t
i
p

t
o
p

h
i
p

t
i

Apéro
Sébasto
Weib
Liszt
Asta Nielsen and Liszt

Mobile

Bandmaster orchestrion page
arm bowing

elegant gesture on side
answering cymbals

couples shuffle the square calmness from tables and stage

circling
into
the
d
e
p
t
h
s

circle turning in square
deeper and deeper
swirlin
g

couples turning
circle turning
yawning chasm
in the squ
are
couples dash their falling sweat into the depths

black pearls

SteP steP to POPular songs HOP

Marie Plancher Marie Planchée

big top hat the boss jigs away
joining in jig jig jig

Stop everyONE says bowing page the dance is DONE

shuffling

slowly the circle sinks in the

square

Bar

The bar is empty

and full of people

nodding harlequins my mild likeness
naive idlers we desire emptiness filling our lifelong need to hide
bar hollow balloon about to burst and will never burst

vi
bleating o
lins a
inescapable pache

is your light body quietly
skirt your still a
still blaze

heads laughter
our being Flat idle
squashed by

bar girls along to faire zizi zozo ZAZA
bleating the song avec

toffs and toffs and toffs and
tarts and tarts and

long empty hours

hours girdling
idle
desire
queue queue queue

Burgeff grün
Mercier
Roederer
Vve Cliquot and Mumm

the champagnes
the tarts
the toughs
all have a price

twirling **Feldwebels Officers** immer lustig bitte is laughing
a profession

tarts toughs stepping day in day out dropping dirty pearls
that you can't sell

soldiers rushing stiff hands stabbing aimlessly
wanting every night again

the CITY started THE DANCE

bourgeois women night-owl through occupied city
dancing after midnight
their ponderous dance
filling the bar a
hollow
b a l l o o n

desire surges uncertain cutting through layers of emptiness

desire surges hollow
breath

IF ONLY

a fruit would fall which was full of fulfilment

HOW

soldiers sit dull desire coagulating into heavy clots
despondency

top hat tornado

until **YOU** are in the middle

spat-out thing from the city **HOLLOW** crazed dance

virgin at whoring daughter of private means perhaps
your clothes hooping wind whooping rushing
cold breaking your bones shell-flake stiff and flowing
rasping-scared disowned
light whip welts hoarse heat screams
lusting screams provocative dance
twirling yourself naked
more naked
more naked
still

Oh the dance won't rape
tornado
inextinguishable

dance of the occupied city
intermediate zone - desires
latent lights
street lamps up and down
lit bar shining in darkness

Dark Street
full of coagulated
CLARITY

nude desire *quivers* in your smile

thin laughter through the street
falling with violins pale in glittering glare
busy
    room
empty
    emptiness
daft
    dance
filling
    falling
dirty
    depraved
feeble comfort

cloakroom with 50 bowlers shakos……

AH

FOLIES BAR

MAMAN you are wonderful
behind the bar as the patrons leave you say
in the melancholy of a grimy opal twilight
Francia play the berceuse from Jocelyn
or
Francia play Gounod's Avé Maria
your face ecstatic in clouds of ether
separation of body and soul
tears rolling mechanically down your face
without effort and as many as you like MAMAN
you are a marvellous tear dispenser
your detached soul floating off with Jocelyn

WITH JOCELYN MAMAN
last note 1 minute or 60 seconds in words sixty seconds later

MAMAN
dignified in grimy batiste
says
C ' e s t t r o p b e a u

The Morning Melancholy

Swirling pallid orchestrion
str__________________etched

Accordion

houses lining up
hoarse street stretched instrument
until long arms stretch it again miniature street

Accordion

faint
flickering
dying
stretched
neck
rising
under pale streetlight

rattling
sign
accompanying
hoarse
pallid
together

CHEZ GERARD
à la réunion des Artisses

nini Columbine whiteness tulle fading
whiteness in pearl-grey street
delicate image

of a saint
as nini goes up she merges into the pallor
or
as street shrinks filthy rag to dirty Columbine costume

square
____ weep on

Aaron Dion

Frost freezes legs to stiff posts crying
standing broken in stretched street
frost freezes the last girl gone

and the last drinker
Cold in a Columbine Costume Cuts through the bar
Cognac I'm freezing all the men are gone
            the room
                  will be full of cold

late
army boots
reduce
      the
city
    to
          d
          i
          s
          t
          a
          n
          c
          e

End of the Inward Circles

The Withdrawal

Limp Lungs

short-winded bellows

screeching pipes

PiPe uPright PuPPet

faltering clock

slow fast fast slow

hours drag

foul wenches

pissed men

cobbles **hollow** **rotten** fruit

gla zing

mechanism slipping

tick tock tick

tock tock

tock

stamping Polish horses rain and sludge

sloB wagon

By

undersized whips Smack

beat of blown out breath

dull bang

desire
pallid pink roses ripen
wither
fa
ll

Asphalt
diluted black watery colours
diluted colours

Hollow Heads
millions of seconds of war fermenting
beat of
broken
things
string snaps
falls violin wood
drenched kindling

old houses

still standing

Helter- Skelter debacle troo **P**s ashen **G**rey

e**X** hau sted

red driving ripping rags locomotives

TB WHEEZE

threads hanging
from sleeves
tattered clothes shabby people

GAWKING

eyes

foreign
and
afraid

Basedow's disease
hollow eyes strangled

requisitioned farmers
requisitioned wenches

all charity meat____________________
no stamp

syphilis *the* clap

Helter- Skelter

plane machine-guns

rattle

sifting the routed army

CRISS CROSS

flight

Rout spouting pus on occupied city

millions of seconds of war fermenting
officers' whips cracking weaker

words growing **waxing** RAGING
murmuring
liPs SeiZing WoRDs
while restless
tick-tock machine-guns BROKEN Cadence

in der Heimat in der Heimat

villages
staggering
sinking

shelldrunk last resistance in ruins

dawn hawks up phlegm
lost heads

thousands of lost heads

Scarecrow standing in sludge **Ruined Rib Cage**

rats ravens

fraying ribs

l i p s
seizing
words

bearing words forward in war's furrows
dragging words into vague monstrance
the moaning

fermenting growing fermenting

GUSHING words

muffling the last weak sound of shells

words **CR**a**SH**ing to **P**iece**S** on **R**o**CK**s

spurt ditch blood

W O R D

state street city soldiers

don't go back Hell

mutter prayers

what will be

lips falter vague murmuring

GROWING

operetta screens reeling pinched smile

LAUGHTER

red

house teetering

breaking plaster

chalk

and yet

VOICE

word voice

waiting hollow

breath

domed room

BANG!

L I E B K N E C H T

who knows
workers and soldiers
might echo

n o w

the doctors the bigshot doctors the bigshot professors don't see
don't hear
draw their homemade wisdom from the Belgischer Kurier
Victory Warsaw Grodno Kovno Brest-Litovsk Bucharest
and now and now
grain from the Ukraine ?
bread
hold out endure
and then
endure
brave Pomerania
victory goes to he who can suffer most
soldiers
Berlin-Baghdad
the kaiser proclaims
(all monarchs proclaim that's their stock in trade)
democratisation of the government
but keep your spirits up
14 points
14 buttons
alle Männer saufen alle Männer saufen

nur der kleine Wilson nicht
growing potpourri of all songs
and then
suddenly

all clocks gather speed
victorious defeated accordion
c'est la valse brune
exhausted beat and restless
sale of helmets bags of coffee machine-guns morphine
the imperial army emporium

Helter

good Catholics anxiously await

VICTÓRY TE DEUM

and the lascivious festivities
emporium buying waiting praying
national quadruple bangers
and the ecstasy the ecstasy
people prepare for ecstasy
course in ecstasy
the nation will be in a delirium of ecstasy
mark my words take care

Skelter

dogs in heat

a race of heroes races of heroes every one
heroism in tablets
heroic syphon

MADELON DE LA **V**ICTOIRE

festivities in perspective Camelot Dionysius

N I H I L

long live nothing

Long live everybody
Long live Max
Long live Mercier
Long live
Martell

Suzon

Wilson waxwork hero
ideology of vegetarian restaurants
man is good etc. etc.
that sort of thing

NIHIL in all languages
ne t'en fais pas
never mind
lig nou niet te klessen
ALLES WURSCHT

To work says the wiseacre

guzzling burgundy

NIHIL

that is the word

destruction

God religion metaphysics churches art brothels mind

don't blather on so

destroy

HAIL THE SENEGALESE

blessed art thou Mary amongst women for thy womb

IS BARREN

Sister Anne can't you see anything yet
no nothing at all dear
words can no longer convey

Oh our longing

for the ruination of all concepts
all hope
all idiocies
the red flood is not rising
the red armies are not growing
and nothing is breaking

and nothing is breaking

if all cathedrals fell

to be Chaos and able to create stone after stone a new house
a new table
jabber
Dionysian delight in first things
Origin
without words   sensual delight

limp lungs   longing   and aimless
because not everything was destroyed

everything   every   thing   was   destroyed

to be Chaos
wall mask no more
this   I – can't – help – it – either
there are no windmills
endless days banal antitheses

always this banging against the wall
we fall   not the wall
the wall of an arsenal

museum arsenal
library arsenal
and all of us arsenals
Amette – Creusot – Schneider – Baudrillart Ltd

Immediacy
is the apex of my desires a lexicon
now
a battering ram alone
a battering ram is the only tool to build
knocking down the makeshift
the caulked
death to the harlequin

Give me something lethal God I want to live

Helter
Skelter
millions of seconds of war fermenting

HollowHeads wanted

Mannequins

lewd fluttering banners
officers offer their sex to the ecstatic mob a monstrance
priests sprinkle holy water
lewd Te Deum of
braying bitches in heat

organ patriotises
magnificat anima mea
all the women from Easylay
we'll have the music you give us

bring on the potpourri

Veni Creator spiritus

c'est lui l'plus beau costo
c'est lui le roi du Sébasto

Tota pulchra es Maria

elle s'appelait Suzanne
elle avait une jambe de bois
de bois de bois

Ave Maris Stella
Vive l'Autrichienne

the Bavarians are withdrawing

VIVE LA BAVAROISE

c'est la jolie Paimpolaise
ma Tonkiki ma Tonkiki ma Tonkinoise

the occupation is over

the occupation begins

potpourri
because
we are

celebrating!

national anthems
national heroes
national colours
everything national

hip hip hoorah for the royal vulva

Vive la nation

ecstasy gentlemen

don't forget ecstasy

cadavers rotting sewers

Tous les soirs grande manifestation patriotique

hopeless skelter
patriotic films
patriotic beer
patriotic lamb

the soldiers are dead

LONG LIVE THE HEROES

to work

why why why

don't blather on so

life ah ah

everything is meaningless

now

crap

LONG LIVE THOSE WHO DIED LIKE DOGS

MAX

!

VIVE

maybe some day

the need will grow so great

all the dykes will break.

Notes...

Most of the following notes are derived from Robert Snoeck's three-volume *Paul van Ostaijen en zijn bezette stad (literaire en zakelijke toelichtingen)* (1975, 1977 and 1984); Gerrit Borgers's *Paul van Ostaijen. Een documentatie* (1996); Jef Bogman's *De stad als tekst; over de compositie van Paul van Ostaijens Bezette stad* (1991); Hansjürgen Bulkowski's notes to his own German translation *Besetzte Stadt* (1991); and my own research online. They are meant as an aid to the reader and are neither exhaustive nor definitive. Although some references are clear, many others are obscure and subject to interpretation, partly because of the passage of time and partly because of Van Ostaijen's tendency to be free in his quotations, at times deliberately subverting them. I have tried throughout to be concise and to avoid any interpretations that seem overly speculative. The titles refer to the different poems or sections of the book.

Dedication

Fantomas A series of silent films directed by Louis Feuillade (1913/1914).

Zigomar Series of films by Victorin Jasset with an eponymous hero (from 1911 on). Among the first feature-length films.

The Iron Prison Third film in Louis Gasnier's series *The Exploits of Elaine*, a follow-up to the famous *Perils of Pauline*, which also starred Pearl White. The series was released in Europe under the title *The Mysteries of New York* (from 1914).

apaches Parisian gangsters, ruffians.

Chéri Bibi French film based on the novel with the same title. '*Fatalitas*' (Latin) is a catchphrase used by the eponymous hero, meaning: 'fatality' in the sense of 'fated/fatal'.

Dieppe o mon pays... Quote from *Chéri Bibi*: 'Dieppe, oh my homeland, I left you a galley slave; a viscount, I see you again.'

Je croyais m'être mis... Quote from *Chéri Bibi*: 'I thought I was wearing the skin of an honest man; but here I am in a murderer's.'

The Last of the Mohicans Novel by James Fenimore Cooper (1826).

Zut Mild expletive (French).

citron nature Pure lemon.

Deo Gratias God willing.

Du rouge pour les lèvres... Dorin lipstick.

De ommegang The Ommegang of Antwerp was an originally medieval pageant.

tête à couper head on the block.

Bayard Giant Giantess Traditional characters in the Antwerp pageant.

O Susanna... The start of a line from a popular German song: 'O Susanna was ist das Leben schön' (Oh, Susanna, isn't life beautiful).

ils en ont tant goûté... Lines from the French drinking song 'Ils sont dans les vignes', meaning 'they ate so much / it made them sick'.

Walzertraum *A Waltz Dream*, an operetta by Oscar Straus (1907).

Lustige Witwe *The Merry Widow*, an operetta by Franz Lehár (1905).

Czardasfürstin An operetta by Emmerich Kálmán, performed in English as *The Riviera Girl* and *The Gypsy Princess*.

Tango Rouge etc. Lines from popular songs. 'Quand je suis grise' means 'When I am drunk'.

rigolo gigolo zigoto Joker, gigolo, oaf.

si tu veux faire... 'If you would like to do a little song', but suggesting 'si tu veux faire une petite balade', 'if you would like to go for a little walk'.

Place Blanche Square in Paris near Pigalle, red-light district.

Privatdozenten An academic title at European, especially German-speaking, universities.

fleurs Houbigant Perfume.

Longchamp, Maisons-Lafitte. Racetracks near Paris.

Lieber Heinz... Dear Heinz, Are you trying to drive me to suicide! I remain as ever Your Hanna.

ne portez pas... 'Don't wear belts too low' (*Femina*, April 1919).

Sehr geehrte... Dear Professor, this case is all the more noteworthy given that the patient's mother was known to have bisexual tendencies and was, in regard to her daughter...

mon chéri... Darling ! It's been 3 weeks since I received any news from you am I dead to you your deeply saddened Felicitée if you no longer love me could you please return my letters and lock of hair...

quand je suis etc. Lines from songs.

L'auto de la mort The Automobile of Death.

drame pol... Police drama 4 parts.

j'ai soupé d'en avoir soupé I am fed up with being fed up.

Threatened City

Visé Liège The first Belgian cities to be attacked by the Germans in August 1914.

Puppchen... Popular German song: 'Sweetie, you are the apple of my eye...'

Heil Dir... German national anthem, 1871-1918, "Hail to Thee in Victor's Crown".

Armee von Kluck... The German First Army, under the command of General von Kluck.

Crump A large artillery shell.

Jef Jef Jef... Flemish satirical song: Jef, Jef, Jef, a zeppelin, quickly creep into the cellar...' (But then in rhyme.)

les hommes au balcon The men on the balcony.

ça va ça viens... Wordplay with several possible meanings, among them something like, 'OK oh come oh come OK'.

un client... A client, ladies, come along.

Recamier Hairstyle popular in the 1910s.

Ah c'est la merde... Ah, it's stuffed, stuff the Germans, stuff everyone.

profitez des beaux... Lines from popular songs.

estaminet A bistro or small café, word in use in English during WWI.

Eendracht... National motto of Belgium (in Dutch): 'Unity makes strength'. In French, 'L'union fait la force'.

Dieu protège... God protect the estaminets.

Valse lente Slow waltz.

Kwatta Popular Dutch brand of chocolate.

De Ruijter... De Ruijter was another brand of chocolate, but the same name, spelt De Ruyter, was a famous admiral in the Dutch Golden Age. The Tromps (father and son) and the De Witt brothers were important figures in the Netherlands in the seventeenth century and stalwarts of Dutch history lessons.

B. S. A. British manufacturer of military and civilian bicycles, the B.S.A. emblem shows three rifles, the source of the bike's French name, *Trois fusils*.

Oberleutnant... First Lieutenant, at your orders.

Gott mit uns God with us.

Kultur A concept of German and specifically Prussian cultural superiority.

Du Volnay An exclusive French wine.

es lebe der Kaiser Long live the Kaiser.

der jute jott (Berlin dialect) Good God.

Sieg Victory.

Garnisonverwaltung Garrison Administration.

Feldlazarett Field Hospital.

3 Etapp. Komm. 3 Rear Comm.
Off. Kas... Off. Mess 4 Reg. Bielefeld.
Soldatenheim Barracks.
Bekanntmachung Announcement.
Der Platzkommandant The Local Commandant.
Beste extra dobbele Styles of Belgian beer: 'Best extra double'.

Hollow Harbour

Kunsten en Ambachten (Dutch) Arts and Crafts.
Garde-Chiourme (French) Prison warder, specifically on a boat with galley slaves.
Dupuys Van Ostaijen probably meant the French artist Dupuis.
leurs lourds marteaux... Their heavy hammers fall rhythmically and tame the metal.
Floris Jespers Belgian painter, brother of Oscar Jespers, who did the woodcuts in the original edition.
flotte petit drapeau 'Fly little flag', a line from a patriotic French song.
Dispache etc. Signs for offices and bars, warehouses, quays, names of ships etc.
C. R. B. Abbreviation: Commission for Relief in Belgium.
Gneisenau, Karthago German warships.
Elvire etc. Names of the pleasure boats moored in the harbour.
Paul Joostens Antwerp painter (1889–1960).
Feldgrau (German) Field grey, the colour of the German uniforms and a term used for the soldiers themselves. Plural: *Feldgrauen.*
Hier gehts... This way to the assembly point for the brave German soldiers.
Nordisk City... A bar.

Brothel

Steinlen French artist particularly known for his posters and drawings of prostitutes and other downtrodden members of society.

je regrette... I'm sorry, sir, war is war.

c'est si difficile... It's difficult, sir.

Vous perdrez... You will lose your high-class customers.

Bapaume etc. WWI battlefields.

Hier schöne... Beautiful young girls here.

Eh là-bas... Hey, over there, granddad, this way.

Zeppelin

good bye Piccadilly... Lines from 'It's a Long Way to Tipperary'.

Beata insula Blessed isle.

fugit irreparabile 'Irretrievable [time] flees', quote from Virgil.

Sous Les Ponts de Paris

Sous les ponts... 'Under the bridges of Paris', title of a 1914 Parisian chanson.

Landsturm Reserves or military unit made of inferior troops, such as older men.

City of Grief

Jaarsma Brand of stove.

Good News

W T Abbreviation for Wireless Telegraphy

Saxe-Coburg-Gotha German dynasty that gave rise to many of Europe's royal families, including those of Belgium and the United Kingdom.

They were Bavarians... The father of the Belgian queen was a Bavarian duke of the Wittelsbach family.

Es lebe Wittelsbach Long live Wittelsbach.

Eisner Kurt Eisner, socialist Bavarian premier, assassinated in 1919.

Music Hall

Pourquoi me... Aria from Jules Massenet's opera *Werther* (1892).

Ridi Pagliaccio Lamentoso from Ruggiero's *Pagliacci* (1892).

mais le plus joli rêve French song, 'but the most beautiful dream'.

La Traviata Giuseppe Verdi's opera (1853).

Jerusalem English song by Stephen Adams, 'The Holy City'.

The Huguenots Opera by Giocomo Meyerbeer (1836).

L'Africaine Opera by Giocomo Meyerbeer (1865).

ce matin j'ai vu... French song.

Aida Giuseppe Verdi's opera (1871).

Samson and Delilah Opera by Camille Saint-Saëns (1877).

The Iron Claw American silent film series starring Pearl White.

Little Jeanne A prostitute in a poem by Blaise Cendrars (1913).

Coco A woman's name and also slang for cocaine.

The Clutching Hand First film in *The Exploits of Elaine*, also the alias of the villain.

Asta Nielsen

Asta Nielsen Danish film actress and star of the silent era.
Sébasto Short for the Boulevard de Sébastopol, a red-light district in Paris.
De profundis clamavi Latin, 'From the depths I cried', first words of Psalm 130.
L'apéro sur... French, 'A drink on the Sébasto', *apéro* is short for *apéritif.*
elle s'approche... 'She approaches unsuspectingly and all at once she leaps.' A variation on two lines from the French song 'La Souris noires' (1912). In the original it is 'I leap'.

Mobile

Mobile The Mobile was a small dance hall in Antwerp.
Marie Plancher... Variants from a popular song about a flat-chested woman.
apache Early twentieth-century dance style, believed to have arisen in the Parisian underworld, with a stylised depiction of violence between the man and woman. (Pronunciation: ah-pahsh).
Feldwebels (German) Sergeants.
immer lustig bitte (German) 'Please, always happy'.

Folies Bar

Berceuse... The lullaby from Benjamin Godard's opera Jocelyn (1888).
C'est trop beau. It is too beautiful.

The Withdrawal

In der Heimat Popular German song: 'At home'.

Liebknecht Karl Liebknecht (1871–1919), German anti-war socialist and member of the Reichstag. Executed after the failure of the Spartacist uprising.

Belgischer Kurier German-language newspaper published in Belgium by the occupier during the war.

14 points U.S. President Woodrow Wilson's 1918 program for world peace consisted of fourteen points.

alle Männer saufen... Parody of the German national anthem: 'all men booze, all men booze, except for little Wilson'.

c'est la valse brune French song.

Madelon de la victoire French song marking the victory, first performed in 1918 by Maurice Chevalier.

Max Adolphe Max, mayor of Brussels.

Mercier Cardinal Désiré-Joseph Mercier.

Martell Brand of cognac.

ne t'en fais pas It doesn't matter.

lig nou niet te klessen Don't rabbit on.

Alles Wurscht It can all go to hell.

Hail the Senegalese Senegalese troops fought with the French army.

Sister Anne... A reference to Perrault's *Bluebeard*.

Amette etc. Amette and Baudrillart were cardinals, Creusot-Schneider denotes the French foundries devoted to military production during WWI.

magnificat anima mea 'My soul does magnify', first words of the Latin Magnificat.

Veni Creator spiritus Hymn: 'Come, Holy Ghost, creator come'

c'est lui l'plus beau costo... Lines from a song: 'He's the best-looking macho, he's the king of the Sébasto.'

Tota pulchra es Maria Hymn, 'You are all beautiful, Mary'.

elle s'appelait Suzanne... Popular song: 'Her name was Suzanne, she had a wooden leg'.

Ave Maris Stella Hymn, '*Hail, Star of the Sea*'.

Vive l'Autrichienne "Long live the Austrian", an ironic phrase used against Marie-Antoinette, who came from Austria. (In French the feminine of *Austrian*, 'Autrichienne', ends with the word *chienne*, 'bitch'.)

Vive la Bavaroise 'Long live the Bavarian', Belgium's Queen Elisabeth came from Bavaria.

c'est la jolie Paimpolaise 'La Paimpolaise' was a popular song (1895) by Théodore Botrel.

ma Tonkiki... Line from the song 'La petite Tonkinoise'.

Tous les soirs... A large patriotic demonstration every evening.

Sources:

JEF BOGMAN'S *De stad als tekst; over de compositie van Paul van Ostaijens Bezette stad* (1991)

GERRIT BORGERS, *Paul van Ostaijen: een documentatie* (1996)

G.J. VAN BORK AND P.J. VERKRUIJSSE, *De Nederlandse en Vlaamse auteurs* on www.dbnl.org

JOSÉ BOYENS, *De genesis van Bezette stad* (1995)

GEERT BUELENS (translation: David McKay), *Everything to Nothing: The Poetry of the Great War, Revolution and the Transformation of Europe* (2015)

HANSJÜRGEN BULKOWSKI'S notes to his own German translation *Besetzte Stadt* (1991)

RENÉ FELIX LISSENS, 'Flemish Poetry' in *Princeton Encyclopaedia of Poetry and Poetics* (1974)

ROBERT SNOECK, *Paul van Ostaijen en zijn bezette stad (literaire en zakelijke toelichtingen)* (three volumes, 1975, 1977 and 1984)

David Colmer
Amsterdam 2016

About Smokestack books

Smokestack aims to keep open a space for what is left of the English radical poetic tradition in the twenty-first century. Smokestack champions poets who are unfashionable, radical, left-field and working a long way from the metropolitan centres of cultural authority. Smokestack is interested in the World as well as the Word; believes that poetry is a part of and not apart from society; argues that if poetry does not belong to everyone it is not poetry.

Smokestack's list includes books by John Berger, Michael Rosen, Katrina Porteous, Ian McMillan, Kate Fox, Martin Rowson, Linda France, Tom Leonard, Judith Kazantzis, Sebastian Barker, Gerda Stevenson and Steve Ely.

Smokestack's growing international list includes books by Bertolt Brecht (Germany), Gustavo Pereira (Venezuela), Rocco Scotellaro (Italy), Heinrich Heine (Germany), Nicola Vaptsarov (Bulgaria), Martín Espada (USA), Francis Combes (France), Andras Mezei (Hungary), Jim Scully (USA), Yiannis Ritsos (Greece), Kristin Dimitrova (Bulgaria), Roque Dalton (El Salvador) and Victor Jara (Chile).

Smokestack's full catalogue is available at www.smokestack-books.co.uk. Contact details: info@smokestack-books.co.uk, 01765 658917; 1 Lake Terrace, Grewelthorpe, Ripon, North Yorkshire HG4 3BU.